Gigi Knits...and Purls

By
Karen
Shalacker

Illustrated
by
Mindy
Dwyer

Includes step-by-step instructions and 8 patterns

acknowledgments

My heartfelt thanks go to: Mary Green and the entire
Martingale family for sharing Gigi with the world. Mindy Dwyer for her amazing artwork,
Ellen Wheat for her skillful editing and guidance, and Elizabeth Watson for her cover and text design.
To Pete, Ella, Robby, Andy, and Malcolm for their love and support.
To Gloria for her encouragement and advice. And to the McKnitters and all of my knitting friends.
Thank you for inspiring me on this unexpected journey.

Gigi Knits . . . and Purls
© 2008 by Karen Thalacker
Illustrations © 2008 by Mindy Dwyer

Martingale®
& COMPANY

Martingale & Company
20205 144th Avenue NE
Woodinville, WA 98072-8478 USA
www.martingale-pub.com

Printed in China
13 12 11 10 09 08   8 7 6 5 4 3 2 1

1745

Library of Congress Cataloging-In-Publication Data
  is available upon request.
ISBN: 978-1-56477-851-2

Mission Statement
Dedicated to providing quality products and service to inspire creativity.

President and CEO: Tom Wierzbicki
Publisher: Jane Hamada
Editorial Director: Mary V. Green
Managing Editor: Tina Cook
Design Director: Stan Green
Production Manager: Regina Girard
Project Manager: Ellen Wheat
Cover and Text Designer: Elizabeth Watson
Copy Editor: Sheila Chapman Ryan

Visit www.gigiknits.com for more!

Contents

gigi knits

Gigi McGreedy was patiently sitting
But her hands were busy with purling and knitting.

Ginger watched closely as Gigi created
A pretty pink scarf as they chatted and waited.

Ginger smiled and made this keen observation,
"I've watched as you knit in surprising locations.

You've made warm mittens at an ice-covered lake.
You've knit dishcloths at a sleepover to help stay awake.

While walking your dog, you knit him a hat.
At the swimming pool you purled a mat for your cat.

Remember the time when you knit in the snow
Or the day at the movies when you stitched a sock's toe?

So I've often wondered and perhaps you'll admit,
Just where is your favorite place to knit?"

Gigi paused for a moment and thought what to say
Then she put down her project and answered this way:

"I think knitting is a truly cool hobby.
I take knitting to school and to the dentist's lobby.

Never in the shower but sometimes in the tub
First a bubble bath with knitting, then a good back scrub.

At the beach I can stitch with my toes in the sand
Or by a crackling campfire after hiking the land.

I can knit in a boat when the fish just aren't biting
And I purl as the sun sets and fireflies are lighting.

I knit with the team on our way to a meet.
We focus our thoughts and prepare to compete.

And in an airport when my flight is delayed,
I stitch and I talk with the friends that I've made.

But of all the places I have rambled and roamed,
My favorite place to knit is at home.

After school when I've conquered those puzzling math facts
And piano's been practiced, I have time to relax.

I plop right down in a comfortable chair
To watch Mom cook dinner, and both of us share

The comings and goings of that busy day
While I knit and treasure the memories we've made."

So Gigi had answered the question at last
But Ginger still had something important to ask.

"I'm not very crafty but it looks like such fun,
Would you mind taking time to show me how it's done?"

So Gigi reached in and from her bag's clutter
Produced needles and soft yarn the color of butter.

"I always have extra," she smiled and replied,
"So an eager friend can give it a try."

learning to purl

needles
(size 8)

knit

behind

purl

in front

Gigi McGreedy first taught you to knit
And you learned how to do it lickety-split.

Now the time has come to learn how to purl
So please get your needles and give it a whirl.

When learning this stitch, the rule you should know
Is that yarn stays in front—not in back—as you go.

So down through the loop, throw the yarn up on top
Now take it to the back, then move it off and stop.

The going may be slow—it might be a disaster.
But don't give up yet, you'll get faster and faster.

Just find a colorful project to do
And we'll find some friends to purl with you.

With Gigi's help, you're sure to succeed.
Practice and patience are all that you need.

scissors

needles
(size 10)

worsted-weight yarn

6

yarn needle

crochet hook
(size 5)

Getting started

I'm so glad you want to learn to purl!

When I first learned the knit stitch, I was so excited! With just the garter stitch, I made scarves, purses, hats, and lots of other things for my family and friends, and even for charity. When I told my grandma I wanted to learn more about knitting, she said it was time for me to learn the purl stitch. I was nervous at first but, with a little practice, I learned to do it! It felt great learning something new, and now I can combine the knit stitch and the purl stitch to make even more kinds of projects.

It's your turn! You did an awesome job learning the knit stitch from *Knitting with Gigi,* and now it's time to purl!

What you'll need

When you're learning to purl, you'll need the same supplies you used in *Knitting with Gigi:* a pair of size 8 knitting needles, some worsted-weight yarn (I recommend yarn that can be machine washed and dried), scissors, a yarn needle, a crochet hook (about size 5), and this book. In addition, you'll need a pair of size 10 knitting needles for a few of the patterns in this book.

By adding a new needle size to your collection, you'll be able to do fun projects with chunkier yarns! You will also want a bag to put your knitting in. You can find all these materials at a nearby craft or yarn store:

1. knitting needles (size 8)
2. worsted-weight yarn
3. scissors
4. yarn needle
5. crochet hook (size 5)
6. knitting needles (size 10)

You'll only need a few things to get started!

7

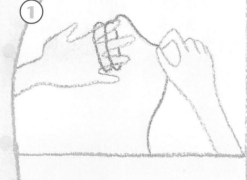

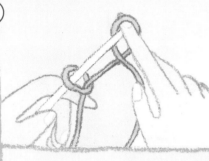

Left-handed knitting

My friend Jen is left-handed and she thought I couldn't teach her to knit because I'm right-handed. She was surprised to learn that lefties can knit just like righties do. But if you're left-handed and have trouble following knitting directions for right-handed people, visit your local yarn store and ask if they have a left-handed knitter who can help you. Knitters love to help other knitters.

With just simple skills, you're a knitter!

Before we learn the purl stitch, let's do a quick refresher on how to knit. If you have any questions, check out my Web site at www.gigiknits.com. There you'll find helpful information and short how-to videos.

1. Making a yarn ball:

If you're working with a skein of yarn, pull the end of the yarn out of the center of the skein and wrap it around your fingers several times. Then slip the yarn off your fingers, and keep winding the yarn around the bunched yarn, crisscrossing it until you've made a big ball. If you are working with a hank of yarn, untie the loose knots and have someone hold the hank while you make a ball, or hang it over the back of a chair. Wrap the yarn loosely so you don't stretch it.

2. Casting on:

Make a slipknot (or any kind of knot) and place it on one of your needles. In your left hand, hold the needle with the slipknot on it. Wrap the yarn around your right index finger until it crosses. Poke the tip of the left needle into the yarn loop on your right index finger, and pull the loop off your finger and onto the needle. Gently snug up the loop, or "stitch." Repeat until you have the number of stitches you need on the needle.

Knitting is a truly cool hobby!

Just remember, "Up, around, down, and off"!

3. Doing the knit stitch:

Hold the needle with the stitches in your left hand. Insert the tip of the right needle up through the first loop on the left needle. Taking the yarn from back to front between the needles, wrap the yarn around the tip of the right needle from back to front. With your right index finger holding down the stitch on your right needle, pull the tip of the right needle and the yarn down through the loop on the left needle. Gently scoot the loop on the left needle up and off the needle. You have created a knit stitch. Continue knitting the stitches until all stitches on the left needle have been knitted onto the right needle.

4. Decreasing stitches:

A knitting pattern may ask that you "knit 2 stitches together" in order to decrease some stitches. To do this, put your right needle into the first 2 stitches on your left needle and knit them together just like you would for knitting 1 stitch.

5. Starting a new yarn ball:

Insert the tip of the right needle into the top stitch on the left needle. Knit the first stitch with the new yarn, leaving a 6-inch tail. Gently tug on the tails of the new yarn and the old yarn so they are snug. Tie the 2 ends together loosely so they won't unravel. You can untie them later when you are weaving in the ends. *(Continued on page 10)*

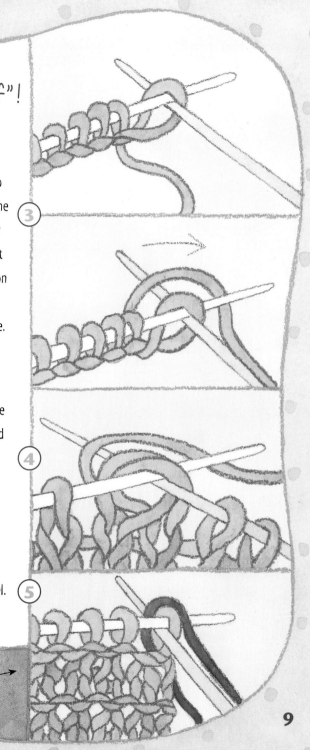

Garter stitch. When you knit every stitch of every row, you are doing the garter stitch. Every 2 rows you knit will form 1 ridge.

Isn't this fun?

9

Finishing a project is so exciting!

6. Binding off:

To weave the stitches of the top edge of your knitted piece together so they don't unravel, you "bind off" the stitches. Knit each of the 2 first stitches from the left needle onto the right needle. With your left needle, gently pull the first stitch on your right needle up and over the second stitch you knitted, and gently scoot the stitch off the needle. You will have 1 stitch on your right needle. Knit 1 more stitch from the left needle to the right needle, and pull the first stitch over the second one as before. Do this until you have only 1 stitch remaining on the right needle. Cut your yarn, leaving an 8-inch tail. Take the last stitch off the right needle, carefully pull the tail through the stitch, and tug gently to secure it.

7. Sewing a seam on a garter stitch project:

Put the edges of your knitted pieces side by side, with the right sides facing you. Line up the garter stitch ridges. Thread your yarn needle with a leftover piece of yarn from your project. Coming from the inside of your project, bring the needle up through the bottom loop on both sides. Pull the needle gently to tighten. On the next ridge up, working on the right side, bring the needle through the loop on one side. Still working on the right side, find the matching ridge on the other side of the seam and bring the yarn through the loop. Gently tighten the yarn. Sew back and forth in this way through every garter stitch ridge until the seam is finished. Make sure the seam is not too tight and not too loose.

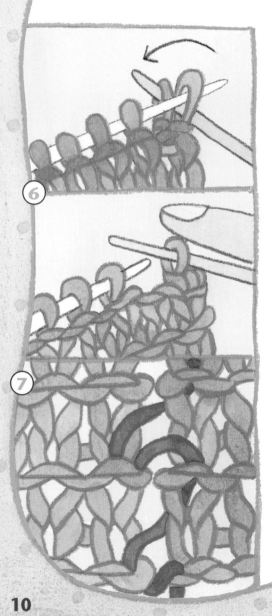

Just practice: you're sure to get better!

I love to knit with friends.

8. Weaving in ends:

When your project is done, turn it inside out. On the inside of the piece, sew (or "weave in") the ends (or "tails") through several stitches with your yarn needle. Secure each end by weaving it around the final stitch a few times before you cut off the remaining tail.

9. Fixing mistakes:

Everyone makes mistakes when they're knitting. But they are usually pretty easy to fix. If there is a hole in your knitting, you can just sew it up when your project is finished. If a stitch has fallen off the needle, just put it back on. If the stitch has fallen off and started to unravel, you can use your crochet hook to reweave the stitch up to the top of your knitting and then slip it back on the needle. Go to my Web site at www.gigiknits.com to watch a video on how to fix an unraveled stitch.

Go to www.gigiknits.com for all sorts of knitting help.

(1)

(2)

(3)

(4)

Ready, set, purl!

Purling is so much fun, but it may feel a little awkward at first. We'll start with a practice project and move on to a real project when you're ready. Just remember to have fun!

Here's how to do the purl stitch:

1. Cast on 20 stitches.

2. Hold the needle with the stitches on it in your left hand.

3. Take the other needle in your right hand and poke the needle down into the first stitch. Your right needle will be in front of the left one, pointing down to the left side.

4. With the yarn in front, put it over the top of the right needle.

"Down, over, back, and off"

For the purl stitch, it might be helpful to say, "Down, over, to the back, off." "Down" refers to step 3. "Over" refers to step 4. "Back" refers to step 5. And "off" refers to step 6.

Purling is a great skill to learn!

Practice until you feel comfortable.

5. With the yarn snug around the point of the right needle, slip the point of the right needle through the stitch and around to the back of the left needle.

6. Gently scoot the stitch up and off the left needle. You now have 1 purl stitch on your right needle.

7. Repeat steps 3 through 6, snugging up each stitch as you go, until all the stitches have been transferred from the left needle to the right needle.

8. Practice doing the purl stitch until you feel comfortable. Maybe it will take 10 rows, maybe 20, perhaps 30. You will then have a knitted piece of all purl rows. A knitted piece of all purl rows is also called garter stitch, just like a piece of all knit rows. In both, 2 rows make 1 ridge.

I'm proud of you for working so hard!

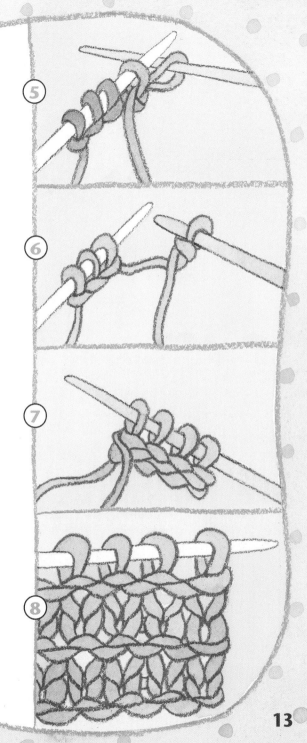

13

It's fun to learn something new!

Now it's time to learn how to combine knitting and purling to make different designs.

It's important to remember that when you are doing the knit stitch, the yarn is in the back of what you are knitting, and when you are doing the purl stitch, the yarn is in the front. It may feel confusing at first, but don't worry; in time you'll get faster and faster.

Here's how to do the stockinette stitch:

Let's continue with our practice project by knitting an entire row and then purling an entire row. When you do this, you are knitting in what is called "stockinette stitch" or "stocking stitch." Unlike garter stitch, where you make ridges of knitting every other row on both sides, stockinette stitch makes your knitting look smooth and flat on the right side and bumpy on the wrong side.

1. For stockinette stitch, knit 1 row and purl 1 row for at least 6 inches.

2. Bind off.

Combining knitting and purling makes your project look great.

Check out my Web site if you have questions.

Here's how to do the basket-weave stitch:

Now it's time to combine the knit and the purl stitches in the same row. That combination is called the "basket weave" stitch. It makes a pattern that reminds me of a checkerboard.

1. Cast on 24 stitches. For our basket-weave stitch, we will use a knit 4, purl 4 pattern. Your tail should be on the lower left of your practice project.

2. At the beginning of the row, knit 4 stitches.

3. Bring the yarn between the 2 needles to the front and purl 4 stitches.

4. Repeat steps 2 and 3 across the row to the end, moving the yarn to the back for the knit stitches and to the front for the purl stitches.

5. Repeat steps 2 through 4 for 3 more rows. You have now done the first 4 rows, or "layer," of the basket-weave stitch. *(Continued on page 16)*

Remember, the yarn goes in front when you purl.

Are you getting the hang of it?

6. On the next row, with the yarn in the front, purl 4 stitches.

7. Bring the yarn between the 2 needles to the back and knit 4 stitches.

8. Repeat steps 6 and 7 across the row to the end.

9. Repeat steps 6 through 8 for 3 more rows. You've completed a second layer of basket weave. See how it looks like a checkerboard?

10. Repeat steps 2 through 9 until you feel comfortable doing the basket-weave stitch. Bind off. Save this practice piece because we're going to use it later when you learn how to sew a seam.

Basket-weave stitch

You alternate knitting and purling across the row, using the same number of stitches for knitting and for purling. The finished piece looks like a checkerboard or a woven basket on both sides.

Doesn't the basket-weave stitch look neat?

The rib stitch makes your project stretchy!

Here's how to do the rib stitch:

Now let's combine the knit stitch and the purl stitch together to make the "rib stitch." When you repeat the rib stitch across the row to make "ribbing," it creates a stretchy, almost elastic piece of knitting, and it looks the same on both sides. For ribbing, the knit stitches and the purl stitches are close together.

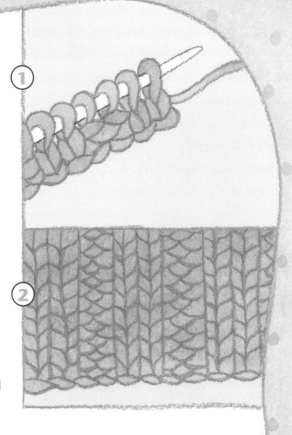

1. Cast on 24 stitches. Knit 2 stitches and purl 2 stitches across the row.

2. On the next row, repeat step 1. After a few rows, you will notice that the ribbing is making your knitting pull together so that the stacks of purl stitches seem to be hiding between the knit stitches. Isn't that neat? Now stretch out your knitting and you will be able to see the purl stitches, too.

3. Practice rows of rib stitch until you are comfortable doing it. Then bind off.

Keep this knitted practice piece handy because we're going to use it to sew a seam.

Rib stitch

You alternate knitting and purling and repeat across the row. The result is stretchy and elastic.

Ribbing is great for hats and cuffs.

The mattress stitch works like magic!

When you make an item with combined knit and purl stitches, you sew up the seam using the "mattress stitch." I like to call it the "magic stitch," because it pulls the seams together like magic. You can use your practice project to practice sewing a seam.

Here's how to do the mattress stitch:

1. Put the edges of your two practice pieces side by side, with the front sides facing you. If you are sewing a long seam, you may want to use safety pins to match up the seams securely before you start to sew.

2. Thread your yarn needle with a leftover piece of yarn from your project.

3. Coming from the back side of your project, bring the needle up and through the bottom corner stitch first on the left piece and then on the right piece. Pull the needle gently to tighten.

4. Still working from the front, find the place where you pulled the yarn through on the left side in step 3. Go back through that hole, inserting the yarn needle from the front to the back.

5. Now insert the yarn needle from the back to the front, 2 stitches up, on the left side. It's easy to count up 2 stitches because the stitches look like the rungs of a ladder. You just find the "rungs," count up 2, and then pull the yarn through from the back to the front. Leave the yarn loose and we will tighten it up in just a bit.

Sewing a good seam makes your finished project look great!

purl project

See www.gigiknits.com for more examples.

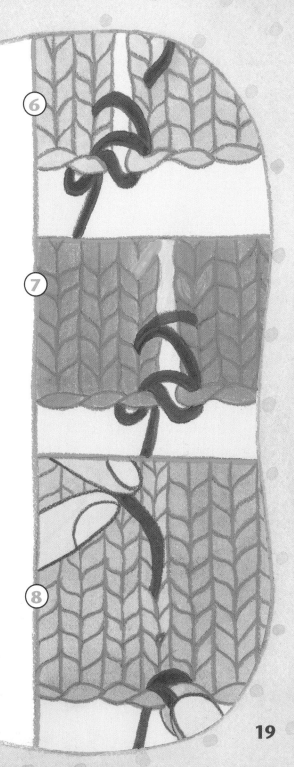

6. Find the place you pulled the yarn through on the right side in step 3. Go back through that hole, inserting the yarn needle from the front to the back. Now insert the yarn needle from the back to the front 2 stitches up to match the left side. Leave the yarn loose.

7. Go back to the left side of the seam and find the hole that was the top rung of the ladder. Go back through that stitch, inserting the yarn needle from front to back. Now insert the yarn needle from the back to the front another 2 stitches up on that same side. Leave the yarn loose and do the same thing on the right side of the seam.

8. After you have worked about 2 inches, it's time to tighten up the seam to see how it looks. Hold the bottom of your seam with your left hand and gently pull the yarn with your right hand to tighten. If you make it too tight, just loosen the seam by pulling the pieces gently to stretch them.

9. Now it's time to sew the rest of the seam. Find the last hole you came out of on the left side and insert the yarn needle in that hole from front to back.

10. Repeat steps 7 and 8 until your seam is all sewn up.

11. When you get to the end of the seam, don't forget to check for a hole in the seam. If you find one, turn your project inside out and mend the hole with the yarn on your yarn needle.

You did it! Good job!

patterns

Gigi McGreedy has patterns for you
With knitting and purling, there's plenty to do.

For friends, for family, for your cuddly pets
You can make them great gifts they'll never forget.

A dishcloth, a scarf, a mat for your cat
A dog coat, a purse, and cute baby hat.

Just go step by step, and use my suggestions
Don't forget my Web site if you have any questions.

And don't be afraid to add your special flair
The personal touches show others you care.

Wherever you go, use your gifts and your skills
To share what you've learned and spread love and good will.

When you knit and purl with zeal and with zest,
You'll be so proud that you're doing your best.

Fancy dishcloth

A fancy dishcloth makes a great gift!

For a friend's birthday, my mom knits a fancy dishcloth, wraps it around a fragrant bar of soap, and ties it with a pretty ribbon. A dishcloth is easy to knit.

This dishcloth is knit with stockinette stitch and has a decorative garter stitch edging. The best yarn for a dishcloth is often called "kitchen cotton" and is 100% cotton. You will need 1 skein.

1. Cast on 35 stitches.

2. Knit 8 rows. You should have 4 garter stitch ridges, and the tail should be on the bottom left of your knitting. You have just knit the border of the dishcloth.

3. Knit 1 row. This row is the first row on the right side of your dishcloth. The right side will have the pattern that you want people to see.

4. On the next row (row 10), knit 5 stitches, purl 25 stitches, and knit 5 stitches. This is the back side of your project, or the side where the pattern does not show.

5. Measure the cast-on edge of your knitting. If your cast-on edge measures 8 inches, then repeat steps 3 and 4 until your piece is 7 inches long. If your cast-on edge is 7 inches long, then repeat steps 3 and 4 until your piece is 6 inches long. Be sure to end with step 4.

6. The tail should be at the bottom left of your project. Knit 8 rows.

7. Bind off loosely and weave in loose ends.

A great idea

This basic square could also be used to make a beautiful blanket. Use any kind of washable worsted-weight yarn. For a baby blanket, knit at least 9 squares, bind them off, weave in the loose ends, and sew the squares together. If each of your friends knits a square or two, you could make a bigger blanket for someone you know who is sick.

Basket-weave scarf

A scarf knit with the basket-weave pattern is fun to make because it creates an interesting design on both sides. I made matching scarves for my mom and dad, and they wore them all winter.

You will need size 10 needles and at least 1 skein of chunky-weight yarn. I used 1 skein that had 164 yards per skein.

1. Cast on 16 stitches.

2. Knit 6 rows for the border. You should have 3 garter stitch ridges.

3. For the next 4 rows, knit 4 stitches, purl 4 stitches, knit 4 stitches, and purl 4 stitches. These 4 rows form the first layer of the basket-weave pattern.

4. For the next 4 rows, purl 4 stitches, knit 4 stitches, purl 4 stitches, and knit 4 stitches. These 4 rows form the second layer of basket weave.

5. Repeat steps 3 and 4 until your scarf is the length you want.

6. For the border, knit 6 rows of garter stitch.

7. Bind off loosely and weave in loose ends.

A fun idea

Knit this scarf with several different colors of yarn. Make the different-colored sections of different lengths, long or short. I like to repeat rows of different colors about every 8 inches or so.

Everyone loves a nice scarf!

Ribbed baby hat

My grandma says that this hat stays on a baby's head better than any hat she has ever knitted. It uses a rib stitch in a really fun way. Her friends at church knit these hats for the hospital nursery. This rib stitch is different from the one learned on page 17. This rib stitch is knit 3, purl 1. You will need size 8 needles and 1 skein of worsted-weight yarn.

1. Cast on 69 stitches.

2. Knit 3, purl 1, and repeat this sequence across the row until there is 1 stitch remaining on the left needle; knit that stitch.

3. Repeat step 2 until the hat is 5 inches long and the tail is at the bottom left corner of your knitting. Now you're ready to shape the top of the hat.

4. On the next row, knit 2 together, and repeat across the row until you have 3 stitches left; knit those 3 stitches together.

5. On the next row, purl across the row.

6. On the next row, knit 2 together across the row.

7. On the next row, purl across the row.

8. On the next row, knit 2 together across the row.

9. Cut your yarn, leaving a 10-inch tail.

10. Thread the tail in your yarn needle. Run the yarn through the remaining stitches on the needle, letting the stitches fall off the needle, and pull the yarn tight. You have formed the top of the hat.

11. With the tail still in your yarn needle, start at the top of the hat and sew the seam together down to the bottom of the hat. You have closed up the seam of the hat. Weave in loose ends.

Every baby should have a cute hat!

Ribbed hat for adults and kids
With chunky yarn and big needles, this hat knits up in no time!

If worn without a brim, this hat is perfect for an adult. If worn with the brim turned up, it's perfect for a child.

You will need size 10 needles and about 150 yards of chunky-weight yarn. I used a yarn that is a blend of wool and acrylic.

1. Cast on 53 stitches.

2. Knit 3, purl 1, and repeat across the row until the last stitch; then knit 1.

3. Repeat step 2 until the hat is at least 8 inches long. The tail should be on the bottom left corner of your knitted piece. Now you're ready to shape the top of the hat.

4. Knit 2 together across the row to the last 3 stitches; then knit 3 together.

5. Purl across the row.

6. Knit 2 together across the row.

7. Purl across the row.

8. Knit 2 together across the row.

9. Cut the yarn, leaving an 18-inch tail. Using your yarn needle, sew the tail through the remaining stitches on the needle, letting the stitches fall off the needle. Pull the yarn tight to close the top of the hat.

10. With the tail still in your yarn needle, start at the top of the hat and sew the seam down to the bottom of the hat. You have closed up the seam of the hat. Weave in loose ends. Note: If you want the hat to have a rolled-up brim, you may not want the seam to show at the bottom. If so, when you are about 1 inch from the end of the seam, sew your seam on the outside of the hat instead of on the inside. This way, the seam won't show when the brim is rolled up.

Ribbed scarf

This scarf can go with the ribbed hat as a set!

This scarf can be made for a child or an adult. Just make it the length you want!

You will need Size 10 needles and about 150 yards of chunky-weight yarn. The yarn I used was a blend of wool and acrylic.

1. Cast on 17 stitches.

2. Knit 3, purl 1 across the row until the last stitch; then knit 1.

3. Repeat step 2 until the scarf is the length you want it (approximately 45 inches long for a child or 55 inches long for an adult).

4. On a row where your tail is on the bottom left of your knitted piece, bind off loosely.

5. Weave in loose ends.

Button purse

This purse is knit in stockinette stitch. You get to make buttonholes for the first time. I love picking out buttons for my knitting projects.

You will need size 8 needles and 1 skein of worsted-weight yarn. I used a cotton-blend yarn. You will also need 3 buttons and a needle and thread to sew the buttons onto the purse. You may want to wait to pick out your buttons until you're done knitting your purse so you can be sure the buttons fit through the buttonholes.

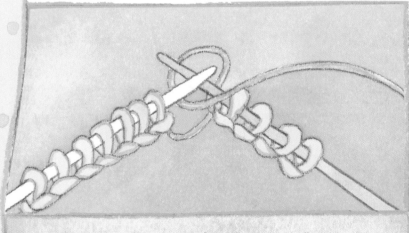

How to make a "yarn over"

A "yarn over" makes a hole in the knitting. Bring the yarn from the back between the needles to the front, and then knit the next stitch as usual. On the next row, knit the yarn-over stitch just like a regular stitch.

To watch a short video on how to make a yarn over, go to my Web site, www.gigiknits.com.

1. Cast on 31 stitches.

2. Knit 4 rows.

3. In this row, we will make our 3 buttonholes. You will need to do 3 "yarn overs" in this row in order to make 3 buttonholes (see box for instructions). For this row: Knit 5 stitches, yarn over, knit 2 stitches together, knit 8 stitches, yarn over, knit 2 stitches together, knit 8 stitches, yarn over, knit 2 stitches together, and knit 4 stitches.

4. On the next row, knit across row, including all yarn-over loops.

5. Knit 3 rows.

6. You are now ready to do a purl row. The tail should be at the lower right corner of your piece, with the wrong side facing you. Purl the entire row.

7. Knit the entire row.

8. Purl the entire row.

9. Repeat rows 7 and 8 until the piece is about 13 inches long. Bind off.

10. It's time to sew up the side seams. Lay the piece flat, with the inside of the purse facing you. The bound-off edge should be at the bottom and the cast-on edge at the top. Fold up the bound-off edge so that about 5 inches of the front side of the piece is showing. There should be about 2 inches at the top that will not be sewn because that part will be folded over and become the flap of the purse. Sew up the side seams.

11. Next, fold over the flap of the purse and figure out where your buttons will go. Under the buttonholes, using pins or yarn, mark the 3 places on the purse where you will sew the buttons. Sew on the 3 buttons. Make sure you sew the buttons onto just the front part of your purse and not the back, too!

12. Weave in loose ends.

13. If you want a shoulder strap for your purse, cast on 70 stitches. Knit 1 row. Then, instead of knitting the next row, bind off. Sew the ends of the strap onto the sides of the purse.

Novelty yarns

You can make this purse extra special by knitting with worsted-weight or chunky-weight "novelty yarn." Yarns that have a lot of texture are often called "novelty yarns." These yarns may look furry or wispy. Some novelty yarns have blobs of yarn called "slubs" woven into the strand. Some even have sequins or other additions to make them sparkle! Follow the pattern and knit about 14 inches, because you need an extra inch at the top for the purse flap.

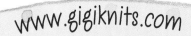

Cat mat

My cat's favorite thing is the mat I made for her. It's just the right size for her to cuddle up on. She loves lying on it in the sun in front of the window.

You will need size 10 needles and 2 skeins of worsted-weight yarn in 2 different colors. I used a yarn that is a blend of acrylic and wool.

Cautionary tale

My veterinarian says that cats should never swallow string. If your cat snags the yarn, mend the mat right away!

1. Cast on 40 stitches in the main color (color A).

2. Knit 20 rows. You should have 10 garter stitch ridges and the tail should be at the lower left of your piece. Cut color A, leaving an 8-inch tail.

3. With your second color (color B), knit 1 row; then purl 1 row.

4. Repeat step 3 two more times. Cut color B, leaving an 8-inch tail.

5. Repeat steps 2 through 4 two more times. You should have 3 stripes of color B.

6. With color A, knit 20 rows.

7. Bind off loosely. Weave in loose ends.

My pets are part of my family!

# Dog coat

The first dog coat I made was for my friend's Chihuahua, Tiny. When it comes to dog coats, one size does not fit all. A coat made for a Chihuahua definitely won't keep a Saint Bernard warm! Just follow my directions and you'll be able to make a coat the right size for the dog in your life.

You will need size 10 needles and at least 1 skein of chunky-weight yarn. If you have a big dog, you will need more yarn. You will also need a tape measure, Velcro fasteners, a sewing needle and thread, and a notepad and pencil. For a small dog I use Velcro circles. For a big dog I use strip Velcro and cut it into pieces. The Velcro circles and strips come in sticky-back and plain, but I always sew the pieces onto the coat so they are secure.

See next page for pattern.

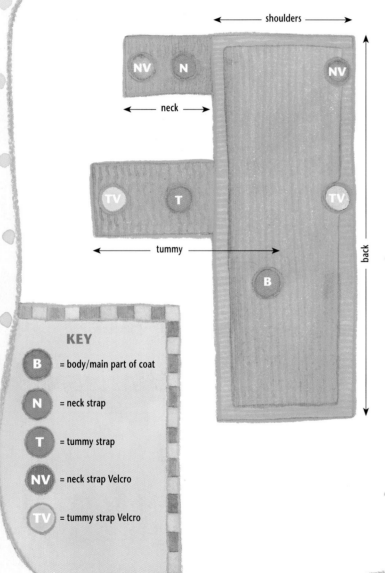

shoulders

neck

tummy

back

NV N

NV

TV T

TV

B

KEY

B = body/main part of coat

N = neck strap

T = tummy strap

NV = neck strap Velcro

TV = tummy strap Velcro

1. Measure your dog in 4 places:

SHOULDERS: on top of his back from the outside of one shoulder blade across to the outside of the other shoulder blade.

BACK: from his neck to about 2 inches short of his tail.

TUMMY: from the midpoint of his rib cage on one side to halfway up his other side.

NECK: on the front, right under his neck, from shoulder to shoulder.

2. For the main body of the coat (B on the diagram), we need to figure out the number of stitches to cast on for your dog. For every inch you measured for the shoulders, you need 4 stitches. For example, my dog's shoulder measurement is 5 inches, so I cast on 20 stitches (5 inches x 4 stitches = 20 stitches). If you have trouble figuring out the math, see my Web site for help, www.gigiknits.com.

3. Cast on the number of stitches from your calculation for your dog's shoulders.

4. Knit 5 rows.

5. Knit 3 stitches, purl across the row until you have 3 stitches left; then knit 3 stitches. This is the back side of the project.

6. Repeat steps 5 and 6 until your piece is about 1 inch shorter than the second measurement for your dog (the back). If your dog's body gets thinner as you go from neck to tail, you may want to knit 2 together at the beginning and ending of a few rows to make the coat fit him better.

7. Knit 4 rows.

8. Bind off.

9. Now it's time to make the garter stitch straps that go around your dog's neck and tummy (N and T on the diagram). Be sure to check your measurements from step 1, because if the straps are too short, they will pull on the Velcro fasteners. For the neck, cast on 5 stitches and knit every row until the piece is the length of the neck measurement. Bind off, leaving an 8-inch tail. For the tummy, cast on 5 stitches and knit every row until the piece is about ½ inch longer than the length of the tummy measurement. Bind off, leaving an 8-inch tail. If your dog is big, you will want to cast on a few more stitches for the straps so they are wide.

10. Using the tails from the bound-off edges and your yarn needle, sew the neck strap (N) and tummy strap (T) to the body (B) as shown in the diagram. The tummy strap should be attached so that it will wrap under the midpoint of the dog's rib cage.

11. Attach the Velcro pieces as shown in the diagram. One piece of the Velcro will be placed on the underside of the strap and the other piece of the Velcro will be placed on the outside of B as shown. Even if the Velcro has a sticky back, sew it in place with a needle and thread to secure.

12. Weave in loose ends.

Some hints

A great way to practice making a dog coat is to make one for your favorite stuffed toy dog. It doesn't take long and then you'll be ready to make one for a real dog in no time!

If your dog is big enough, you may need to make 2 straps for under his belly.

Check out my Web site for a pattern for dog leg warmers.

Gigi's Kindness Corps

Here's a chance to use your knitting to help other people!

You're invited to join Gigi's Kindness Corps. Your assistance is needed as never before.

We knit for folks who are in need. Our mission will cover the globe with good deeds.

But there's no need for Super Boy or Wonder Girl. For it's kids just like you who will save the world.

When people are hurting, the Corps will be there To help soothe their troubles and show them we care.

When thousands of needles are clicking away, Then hope and compassion will carry the day.

So do not delay, your spirits will soar When you sign up to join Gigi's Kindness Corps.

Did you know there are people all over the world who need our help? That's why I'm inviting you to join Gigi's Kindness Corps™. As members of GKC, you can use your knitting skills to create useful items for people in need. You'll find on my Web site complete information, a sign-up form for GKC, and patterns for knitting projects (www. gigiknits.com). I guarantee that your service in Gigi's Kindness Corps will be filled with fun and friendship, so let's get started!

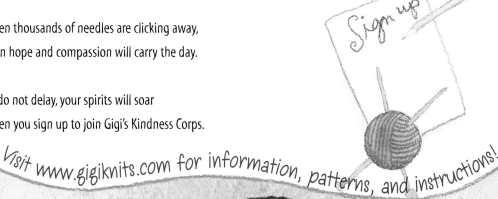

Visit www.gigiknits.com for information, patterns, and instructions!